The plants grow in giant greenhouses called Biomes, which look like big bubbles.

Biomes

We're walking down past flags and flowers. The Biomes look bigger and bigger as we get closer.

A Day at the Eden Project

Written by Kate Petty

Photographs by Ley Honor Roberts

Contents

Collins

Arriving

We're at the Eden Project in Cornwall.
It's a special place with plants from all
over the world.

The jungle

We go inside the first Biome and now we're in the jungle.
It's warm, wet and green in here.

We can hear water rushing and dripping.

There's a jungle house made from wood, grass and bamboo.

grass

wood

bamboo

Rubber plants and pineapples are
growing here.

rubber plants

pineapples

Did you know that chocolate comes from trees? It's made from cocoa beans which grow inside big orange pods.

d chocolate

the tropical
d the plants they
enefit the cocoa fa
late eaters.

← →
70m   90m

cocoa pods

a banana
plant

Bananas are growing high up in bunches. We wish we could pick one!

a bunch of bananas

Oranges and lemons

The next Biome is cooler.

oranges

It smells lovely. We can see oranges and lemons growing on the trees.

lemons

Here are some little pigs under the cork oak trees.
They are made of wood from the trees.

cork oak tree

The bark is made into corks for bottles.

grapes

vines

We can see bunches of grapes hanging from the vines.

So much to see

We have our packed lunches outside. We've got spinach in our sandwiches –
just like the spinach growing behind us.

spinach

There's so much to see.
There's an enormous bee and
a giant made from metal.

Goodbye!

Goodbye, Eden Project.
We can't wait to come back again.

Eden Project map

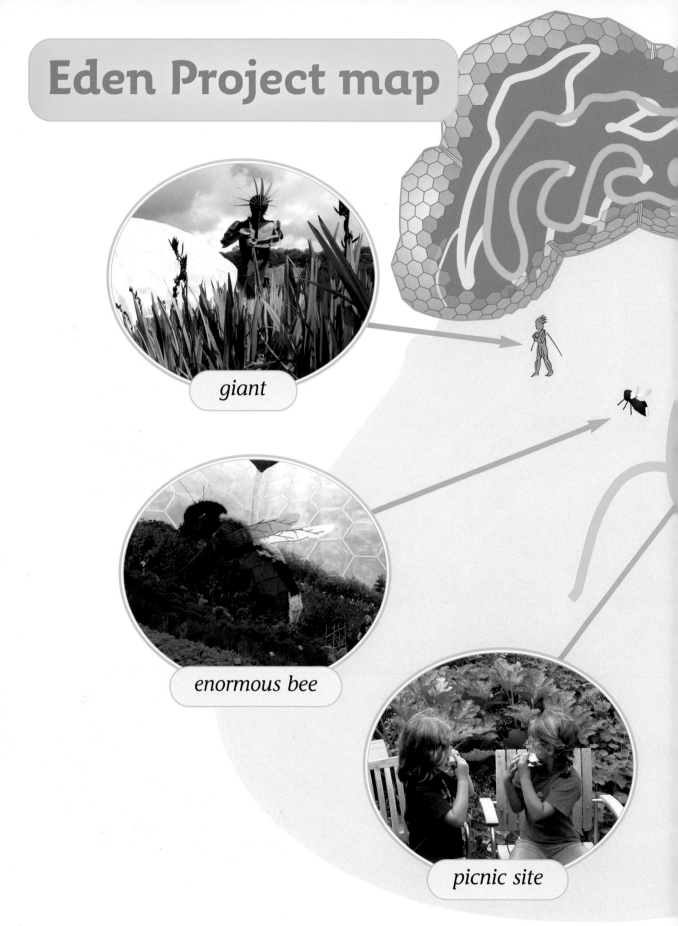

giant

enormous bee

picnic site

Tropical Biome

Mediterranean Biome

path to Biomes

visitors' centre

entrance

23

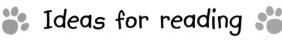 Ideas for reading

Written by Linda Pagett B.Ed(hons), M.Ed
Lecturer and Educational Consultant

Learning objectives: Read recounts and begin to recognise generic structure, e.g. ordered sequence, use of sequencing words; identify simple questions and use text to find answers; locate parts of text that give particular information; identify the common spelling pattern for the long vowel phoneme ee; explain views to others in a small group and decide how to report the group's views to the class.

Curriculum links: Geography: Where in the World is Barnaby Bear?; Science: Growing plants, plants and animals in the local environment

High frequency words: with, did, made, so, much, back, again, could, one, here, down, green, red, from, our, us

Interest words: Eden Project, Cornwall, Biomes, bamboo, cocoa, chocolate

Word count: 256

Getting started

- Look at the cover and read the title together. Leaf through the book looking at the pictures to decide what the Eden Project could be about. *Has anyone been there? What did you see there?*

- Ask the children what they think they might find at the Eden Project, using the illustrations to help them.

- Together, read pp2–3 to introduce the idea of the Eden Project and discuss the Biomes. Extract the fact that plants found in the Project are normally found in other countries.

- Skim through the rest of the book reading the interest words together, e.g. *Biomes, bamboo,* and discuss what is happening in the pictures.

Reading and responding

- Ask the children to read independently and quietly to p13, using a range of strategies when they encounter a challenging word. Remind them of the interest words that you looked at together, and ask them to look out for them.

- Listen in on each child reading aloud, praising and prompting good use of strategies.